D0183957

Falkirk **Community** Trust

MEADOWBANK LIBRARY
2A STEVENSON AVENUE
POLMONT
FK2 0GU
TEL: 01324 503870

Bo'ness
01506 778520

Bonnybridge
01324 503295

Denny
01324 504242

Falkirk
01324 503605

Grangemouth
01324 504690

Larbert
01324 503590

Meadowbank
01324 503870

Slamannan
01324 851373

2 2 JUN 2018

2 1 AUG 2018

2 6 MAR 2020

Falkirk Community Trust is a charity registered in Scotland, No: SC042403

This book is due
for return on or
before the last date
indicated on the
label. Renewals
may be obtained
on application.

What Dogs Do When You're Not Looking

MARY COLSON

raintree
a Capstone company — publishers for children

FALKIRK COMMUNITY
TRUST

Raintree is an imprint of Capstone Global Library Limited, a company incorporated in England and Wales having its registered office at 264 Banbury Road, Oxford, OX2 7DY – Registered company number: 6695582

www.raintree.co.uk
myorders@raintree.co.uk

Text © Capstone Global Library Limited 2017
First published in paperback in 2018
The moral rights of the proprietor have been asserted.

All rights reserved. No part of this publication may be reproduced in any form or by any means (including photocopying or storing it in any medium by electronic means and whether or not transiently or incidentally to some other use of this publication) without the written permission of the copyright owner, except in accordance with the provisions of the Copyright, Designs and Patents Act 1988 or under the terms of a licence issued by the Copyright Licensing Agency, Saffron House, 6–10 Kirby Street, London EC1N 8TS (www.cla.co.uk). Applications for the copyright owner's written permission should be addressed to the publisher.

Edited by Helen Cox Cannons
Designed by Philippa Jenkins
Picture research by Morgan Walters
Production by Laura Manthe
Originated by Capstone Global Library Limited
Printed and bound in India

ISBN 978 1 4747 3850 7 (hardback)
21 20 19 18 17
10 9 8 7 6 5 4 3 2 1

ISBN 978 1 4747 3854 5 (paperback)
22 21 20 19 18
10 9 8 7 6 5 4 3 2 1

Falkirk Community Trust	
30124 03093633 2	
Askews & Holts	
J636.7	£8.99
MK	

British Library Cataloguing in Publication Data
A full catalogue record for this book is available from the British Library.

Acknowledgements
We would like to thank the following for permission to reproduce photographs: All photographs by Capstone Studio: Karon Dubke.

We would like to thank Caroline Kisko, Secretary and Communications Director at the Kennel Club for her invaluable help in the preparation of this book.

Disclaimer
All the internet addresses (URLs) given in this book were valid at the time of going to press. However, due to the dynamic nature of the internet, some addresses may have changed, or sites may have changed or ceased to exist since publication. While the author and publishers regret any inconvenience this may cause readers, no responsibility for any such changes can be accepted by either the author or the publishers.

Some words are shown in bold, **like this**. You can find out what they mean by looking in the glossary.

CONTENTS

Hello!

Woof, woof! That's dog talk for "Hello!" I'm so excited to meet you! I'm Ted and I'm going to tell you all about myself. You will learn about the crazy things I get up to when my owners aren't at home! I may look soft, cuddly and cute but deep down I'm pretty wild!

I'm your best friend

Matt, Beth, Mum and I make a great team. We're best friends and we look after each other. I'm very **loyal**.

When they get up, everyone comes and pats me to say "Hi!" Before they go to work and school, they give me fresh water, my dry food and some meat. I get some dog biscuits, too, if I'm lucky. Yum!

I'm a top explorer!

Bye, see you later!

When Mum and the kids have left, I wander around the house. I like to explore. I'm very clever and learn quickly. I can open the doors by jumping up and twisting the handles. I like to sniff around in cupboards, too. Let's see how messy Beth's bedroom is today...

Super sniffers

If I may say so myself, I have an amazing nose! I'm much better at smelling than you are. My nose has got millions of **scent glands**. I can sniff out danger as well as friends and treats.

I have great whiskers, too! They help me find my way in the dark.

Ooh! What's that under the sofa? Crunchy!

Listen up!

Woof! What's that outside?

Dogs have excellent hearing – much better than humans do. I can sometimes hear things from more than 1.6 kilometres (1 mile) away. I can even tell when the family are on their way home before they arrive. I sometimes lean my head to the side to hear better.

Warning bells

Grooooowl! I can hear another dog! Why is he on my **patch**? The cheek! Woof! Woof! There, I think I scared him off.

I use lots of different noises to show my feelings. I **yelp** if I'm hurt and **whimper** if I'm sick. When I'm really cross, I growl.

Don't scare me!

Just like you, I don't like being scared. I react to defend myself, my family and my **patch**. I bark loudly or **whine**. If I can see danger, my eyes narrow. I'm totally ready to attack. My ears go up and so does my tail. That's my **signal** for "stay away"!

A very quick clean

Slurp! That's better! I like to clean any bits of food from around my mouth and dirt from my paws. That's about it for my washing **routine**!

Matt and Beth think I smell stinky sometimes but I like my smell. Mind you, it is fun when they give me a bath. Afterwards, Mum uses her hairdryer on me and I feel like a doggy model!

Chewing machine

Look what Beth has left under the sofa – her slipper!

I love to chew on things. I like **gnawing** on **rawhide**. Rawhide helps to keep my jaws and teeth strong. Usually, I prefer to chew real food but, until teatime, Beth's slipper will do!

Playing is practising

Just like you, I love to play. Playing keeps me fit and strong. I like playing with my toys. The best ones make a noise. I like squeaky toys because it's like hunting. I pretend I'm chasing my **prey**. This also helps me practise keeping my home safe.

Sometimes, I bark when I play to show that I'm having fun.

Walkies!

Woof! Woof! Mum, Beth and Matt are home! Great! Now I can go for my walk. I hope we go to the park. I can run around the park when they let me off the lead. They throw balls and I race to catch them. If I do a really good catch I get a tasty treat!

When you go to sleep...

Yawn! I get sleepy in the evenings. When Mum, Matt and Beth go to bed, they always say "Night, night. Don't wake us up!"

I settle down in my bed. I don't go straight to sleep, though. I am watching and listening...

What's that noise? There it is again. Right, I'm ready. Woof! Woof! Woof!

How wild is *your* dog?

1. What does your dog do when it hears a noise outside?

a) It growls for a minute then just ignores it.

b) It runs and hides behind the sofa.

c) It barks like crazy.

2. What does your dog do with noisy toys?

a) It pushes them away.

b) It whines because it doesn't like the noise.

c) It grips them with its sharp teeth and won't let go.

3. What does your dog do when you leave your shoes out?

a) It picks them up and carries them to your room.

b) It sniffs them then curls up with them in its basket.

c) It chews, bites and gnaws them to shreds!

4. What does your dog do when you let it off the lead?

a) It sniffs the ground and eats some grass.

b) It stays close to you for safety.

c) It races off, happy to be running.

To find out how wild your dog is, check the results on page 32.

Glossary

gnawing chewing really hard on something

loyal faithful and true to someone or something

patch territory; area where something lives or roams

prey animal hunted and eaten by another animal

rawhide skin of a cow that can be eaten

routine regular things a person or animal does

scent glands special organs in the body that make smells

signal action which gives some information or a message

whimper make a quiet, crying sound

whine moan, complain

yelp cry out in pain

Find out more

Books

All About Dogs and Puppies, Anita Ganeri (RSPCA, Scholastic, 2014)

Designer Dog Projects (Pet Projects), Isabel Thomas (Raintree, 2015)

Dogs (Animal Family Albums), Paul Mason (Raintree, 2013)

Ruff's Guide to Caring for Your Dog (Pets' Guides), Anita Ganeri (Raintree, 2013)

Websites

www.thekennelclub.org.uk
The Kennel Club is an organization that aims to protect and promote the health and wellbeing of dogs. Their website contains lots of fascinating information about dogs.

www.rspca.org.uk
The Royal Society for the Prevention of Cruelty to Animals has lots of important information about pets and pet care.

Index

Quiz answers:

Mostly As: Your dog is very chilled! He's not bothered by anything much. He's happy to do his own thing in a very calm way.

Mostly Bs: Your dog likes the quiet life. He would rather hide away than face up to danger. He's supposed to protect you, not the other way around!

Mostly Cs: You clearly have the wildest dog in town! He'll take on anyone and anything!